I0164698

# The Power of Visualization

# Meditation Secrets
# That Matter The Most

# Sri Vishwanath

www.soulpowermagic.com

ISBN: 978-0-9847563-1-5


www.soulpowermagic.com

**You can contact the author at vish@vish-writer.com or vish@soulpowermagic.com
You can also reach him at his USA number
at 2138142680.**

Also by Sri Vishwanath

1) **Shakti** : Revealed- How You Can Feel Great In Sixty Seconds Flat.

2) **The Secret of Getting Things Done** : Think Less Achieve More.

3) **The Power of Vedas** - The Spiritual Guide That Has Been 5500 Years In The Making.

4) **Reason why people come into your life**- A powerful story that reveals answers to life's most challenging problems.

5) **How to Meditate effortlessly-** Deep Meditation Experience to feel great,enjoy your own company  and take faster decisions in life.

6) **Hijacking the Mind** – 24 Mental Triggers to Make you Feel Great

7) **Give Up --- Your Excess Baggage** 24 Simple Mind Exercises That Great Men & Women Effectively Use Every Single Day.

# Dedication

TO Sri KRISHNA, SRI RAMAKRISHNA, SWAMI
VIVEKANANDA & SHARADA DEVI

## Table of Contents      PgNo

## Introduction

"People who soar are those who refuse to sit back, sigh and wish things would change. They neither complain of their lot nor passively dream of some distant ship coming in. Rather, they visualize in their minds that they are not quitters, they will not allow life's circumstances to push them down and hold them under"

Lets put it this way. **You can have anything that you want if you can master the art of visualization.** Now visualization is not like the law of attraction or any other similar law that you might have read. Visualisation is a mind tool that anyone can access. It is not mystical. It is based on your ability to access fields which you own but are not aware of. Visualization is not complex neither is it simple. It requires you to master the fundamentals of effortless meditation. It does not matter if you are a beginner to meditation or you have spent 20 yrs in meditation. This little book will teach you to visualize like the masters. I have put together five special exercises at the end of the book which will help you to take your life to the next level

I hope you enjoy the book and I look forward to hearing from you.

Lets begin.

## What is Effortless Meditation?

■■■■■■■■■■■■■■■■■■■■■■■■■■■■■■■■■■■■■■■

*You may meditate on whatever you like but I will meditate on the heart of a lion.*

Swami Vivekananda

■■■■■■■■■■■■■■■■■■■■■■■■■■■■■■■■■■■■■■■

There is only one skill in this world which can help you reveal your true potential. Every other skill will fall short in helping you remember your real nature. Before I reveal this unique skill I want to tell you a story.

This is a story about a pregnant lioness who gave birth to a baby lion before suddenly dying while attacking a flock of sheep. Taking pity on the cub, the sheep brought the young lion up. The lion ate grass and not meat, and bleated like a sheep. In time, it became a big, full-grown lion, but the lion still thought it was a sheep.

One day another lion came in search of prey, and was astonished to find that in the midst of this flock of sheep was a lion, fleeing like the sheep at the approach of danger. He tried to get near the sheep-lion to tell it that it was not a sheep but a lion but the poor animal fled at his approach. However, he watched his opportunity, and one day found the sheep-lion sleeping.

He approached it and said, *"You're a lion."*

*"I'm a sheep,"* bleated the other lion.

The lion dragged him towards a lake and said, *"Look! There is my reflection and yours."*

Then came the comparison. The sheep-lion looked at both reflections, and realized he was indeed a lion. He let out a mighty roar. The bleating was gone, never to return.

**Big Secret No 1: Truth is obvious. You don't have to go through a learning process to experience the highest truth. The revelation is instant and immediate.**

A sheep can't become a lion. We all know that. It's only a lion which has ignorantly adorned the 'sheep mindset' that can remember its real nature and regain its lost kingdom. What made the sheep/lion remember its real nature? Was it seeing its own reflection in the water or was it something else? The sheep/lion might have seen its reflection in water many times before it met the other lion, yet it continued to bleat like a sheep. So what really triggered the magical transformation in the sheep/lion that day?

It's a mysterious ten letter word called "Meditation"

Meditation like the word God is the most misunderstood word in the English dictionary. Though there are tons of literature and thousands of certified teachers teaching various methods of meditation, only a handful of human beings can really "meditate." What is it that profound men and women attain through meditation that others can't or don't?

**Big Secret No 2**: You don't meditate to "know"; rather you meditate because you "know."

The biggest fallacy told about meditation is that if you sit in a quiet place, close your eyes and focus on a desired object or image for a while, something magical will happen. This is all nonsense. Nothing happens.

Consider an example:

If a donkey admires a horse and wants to become like a horse, do you think it can become a horse by meditating on the image of the horse?

No! It simply can't become like a horse by so thinking of itself. We've seen earlier that you can only become something which you are. You can never become something which you aren't. The donkey can never become a horse because it isn't a horse; it's a donkey.
Consider a different scenario. Assume that a horse has forgotten its real nature and assumed

the mind-set of a donkey. Now the horse wants to regain all the characteristics of his kind. Would the transformation happen if it meditates on the image of a horse?

**Big Secret No 3**: Like attracts like. Period. Reread this truth until it becomes seared in your mind.

There's only one way for the horse to reclaim its true character. It has to acknowledge its real identity. *"I am a horse and I have all the characteristics of a horse. It doesn't matter if I had assumed the donkey mind-set for decades. **Time can't eliminate the essence of my being. I was, I am, and I shall be a horse always.**"*

As the horse contemplates these words a strange power overtakes him. The light of transformation pierces the veil of the donkey mind-set and for the first time after many years of ignorance the horse is able to reflect upon its own existence without any effort or imagination. The soul of the horse had merged into the spirit of the other horse it was meditating on. Like had attracted like.

**If you want to become like a Buddha you have to meditate on the image of the Buddha through the mind of the Buddha.**

That's the only way. You can't use your own mind to focus on the greatness of Buddha. Say to yourself: "I admire Buddha because I see in him all those characteristics which appear to be latent in me. My current level of consciousness is what stops me from expressing my real nature. I come from that same source which produced the great Buddha. Time can't eliminate the essence of my being. I was, I am, and I shall always retain the core characteristics of a Buddha. **That which fire cannot burn, the wind cannot dry, the water cannot wet I am that force. That power, that love, that peace called Buddha exists in me and I in Him**."

This is the biggest lesson to learn if you want to plump the depths of your consciousness. Start by acknowledging that you're complete. All those characteristics which you're chasing or which you admire in others already exist in you in a "seed" form.

Meditation is the process which lends power to transform this seed into a full grown ripe fruit. There's nothing magical happening in meditation, just like there's nothing magical about a seed which in time grows into a fruit.

Meditation is all about acknowledging your greatness. It reminds you that you don't possess the fruit right now but you own the seed. This lends you power. It gives you ownership. Why do human beings suffer? Our minds are trained to blindly pursue our desires. In our endeavor to attract the desired results we fail to acknowledge the power of the abilities which we already own and which would eventually lead us to our objectives. **That which we seek we already own**.

If you're seeking a million dollars you should be aware that you already possess the ability to become rich. This ability is the seed to meditate upon with complete earnestness. Tremendous power will emerge, filling you with mind-blowing ideas to achieve your goals. The ability to become rich is a characteristic within you which you had ignored in your pursuit of becoming rich. Acknowledge it, meditate on it, and you will become wealthy in time.

If you're seeking love be aware that you already possess the ability to be loved. This spirit of love is what you should meditate on. Contemplate on this magic of love. Let your whole being whisper the silent language of love. Meditate on the mind of Christ or any other great figure whom you love. Feel the love surging up from your being. Watch it envelop and spread across the whole universe. That warm feeling has its origin from the same source that prompted you to seek love. The love that you were seeking and the love that you had the capacity to express all come from that same source. It's only the medium through which it's channeled that differs. In the former it's routed through your lover; in the latter it originates from you.

The love which you seek is already yours. Simply express your love in every possible manner and the seeker will merge with the sought just as the thinker merges with the thought. You'll find your true love or your true love will discover your spirit.

## The Meditation Mind-Set

We don't suffer because of the problems, struggles and failures arising in our life. We endure pain because of one and only one thing. Our inability to hold on to something greater than our current difficulties.

When faced with a major obstacle we forget our real strengths. We crumble. When down and out, we need infinite strength. But when we need it the most we don't have any means to access it. Why?

**Big Secret No 4:** Truth can't be seen. Truth can't be heard. Truth can't be touched. Truth can't be felt. If it could it would cease to be a truth.

Truth is the source of all strength and power. Truth is the source of everything that shines through and outside of us. We live with truth and truth with us. It's vital to know and experience the grandeur of truth and the means through which it reflects its power through our persona.

Consider an example:

Two men set out on an expedition to visit the Seven Wonders of the World. Their first stop was the Taj Mahal in the Indian city of Agra. For centuries, the Taj Mahal has inspired poets, painters and musicians to try and capture its magic in word, color and song. One of the most flawless architectural creations of the world, it was built in the memory of the beautiful Mumtaz Mahal, who won the heart of the Mughal prince, Shahjahan. Since the 17th century, travellers have crossed continents to come and see this ultimate memorial to love, and its incomparable beauty has touched many a soul.

When the two men visit Taj Mahal the first gentleman is absolutely stunned with the energy, purity and brilliance radiating from the architectural memorial built in pristine marble. He's speechless and in awe. The second man, however, isn't that impressed. He's having a terrible stomach problem that day and was going through a major crisis in his relationships. As the two men leave the Taj Mahal the first man carried with him wonderful memories of this piece of exquisite art while the second had no extraordinary reminiscences as a result of his disturbed mind.

Both men saw the splendor of Taj Mahal through their eyes. One was stunned and the other indifferent at most. Why was the second man not able to appreciate the beauty of the Taj Mahal?

**We see through our eyes but we react through our mind. That which we see outside is only a dull reflection of our inner state of mind.**

Truth can never be found outside of ourselves. Taj Mahal isn't the epitome of beauty. The marvel, the splendor and the purity of the Taj Mahal can only radiate from a like mind.

Everything that we see we observe through our mind.

Everything that we hear we listen through our mind.

Everything that we touch we experience through our mind.

Everything that we feel we reflect through our mind.

The external world can only be perceived through our mind and the mind can't lead us to truth. Why? The mind is vigorous at one time and weak at another because it can be acted upon by anything and everything. The thoughts which you think today might undergo a radical change tomorrow based on some future experience.

**Everything that you see, hear, touch or feel is subject to change. Anything which is subject to change can't be the source for experiencing the truth**.

The first test of truth is it can't be subject to change. It can't be acted upon by anything. No force is more powerful than the force of truth.

**Why cannot truth be subject to change?** If truth is subject to change then it ceases to be the truth, and the force which brings about the change becomes the truth. Since this force is more powerful than the previous force, it follows then that the force which can't be acted upon by anything is the ultimate truth. This is the truth we have to meditate on, the one which can't be perceived by our senses. That truth which cannot be seen, which cannot be heard, which cannot be touched and which cannot be felt, that truth we have to all meditate on.

## The Divine Lens

*The pure and simple truth is rarely pure and never simple.*

– Oscar Wilde

Meditation is a force. It's a state of being which every human being can experience. The highest reward of meditation is the supreme degree of alertness which meditation generates. This awareness can facilitate a deep and powerful connection with every single living and non-living object in the universe.

When you meditate you lose the capacity to be selfish. You no longer possess the ability to hate anyone. You find it extremely difficult to restrict your love to only your closed ones. When you meditate you see through your eyes but you don't react through your mind.

The tree might appear to be different from the bird, the sky might appear to be different from the moon, a mother might appear to be different from her son. Yet this differentiation doesn't affect your ability to experience the force which transformed the tiny seed into a gigantic tree, the force which evolved into the bird's wings, the force which holds the whole galaxy of stars and planets in this vast and boundless azure, the force which lights up the dying night with a cheerful moon like face, the force which hypnotizes the mother to love her son and the son to acknowledge the motherly love. That force when you meditate on you longer separate the good from the bad, the wicked from the virtuous, the ignorant from the knowledgeable.

Imagine that you possess this uncanny ability to recognize that one force which became the good in one person and the bad in another, the force which took the form of a wise being in one soul and a crooked personality in another. Would this ability help you lead a better life, resolve your current conflicts, help you think clearly, and above all guide you in the path of truth? You will be stunned with the power that will emanate from your being once you master this grand skill and I will reveal to you the specific way of meditation to begin a new way of being.

### The Way to Meditate

■■■■■■■■■■■■■■■■■■■■■■■■■■■■■■■■■■■■■■■■■■■■■

*He who in the midst of intense activity finds the greatest calmness and in the midst of great*

*peace discovers intense activity is a true seeker
of truth.*
   – Krishna to Arjun in the Bhagavad Gita

■■■■■■■■■■■■■■■■■■■■■■■■■■■■■■■■■■■■■■■■■■■■

Meditation isn't an activity or exercise which
you choose to do during certain times of the
day. Meditation is like breathing. If you stop it
you lose your awareness and connection with
the life force.

How did Krishna meditate? How did Buddha
meditate? How did Christ meditate? What did
they know or what did they become that
propelled them to such amazing heights of
reverence, worship and love?

**The Three Instruments of Knowledge**

All our actions are guided by knowledge. The
lowest instrument of knowledge is instinct.
You'll find this predominant in animals, but
many human actions are also guided by
instincts such as eating, sleeping, and making
love. The sphere of action is very limited in
instinct and so the experience which one draws
out of it is restricted.

The next instrument of knowledge is reasoning.
The ability to discriminate between good and
bad, and to make choices in life, is only
possible because of our reasoning skills.
Reasoning enlarges our scope of action and
gives us a broader field to shape and work out
our experiences. However, the power of

reasoning comes with its own set of boundaries and limitations.

■■■■■■■■■■■■■■■■■■■■■■■■■■■■■■■■■■■■■■■ı
## Logic becomes argument in a circle

Take, for instance, the very basis of our perception of matter and force. What is matter? That which is acted upon by force. What is force? That which acts upon matter. See the relationship of one idea depending on the other. You find a mighty barrier before reason beyond which reasoning can't go; yet our minds always feels impatient to get into the region of the infinite beyond. This universe, which our senses feel or our mind thinks, is but one atom of the infinite projected on to the plane of consciousness. It's placed within that narrow limit of potential reason.

*Therefore, there must be some other instrument to take us beyond and that instrument is called: Inspiration.*

Swami Vivekananda

■■■■■■■■■■■■■■■■■■■■■■■■■■■■■■■■■■■■■■ı

What reason can't help us understand is brought to light through the medium of inspiration. The first test of inspiration is that it shouldn't contradict reason; rather it should fulfill it.

Krishna was inspired. Buddha was inspired. Christ was inspired and so were all the men and women we revere. They simply lived their lives and their character became their message. When they spoke they made no attempt to influence the minds of their disciples. Rather they spoke of something beyond, the source of all manifestation, which was present in every being. This is the form of a latent force which every individual can discover for themselves and thus experience a surge of strength, courage and hope.

Inspiration is a way of life. It provides us with an opportunity every moment to feel and express the greatness and grandeur of this marvelous force. Inspired beings don't discriminate between good and bad; Instead they discover new and unknown ways to uplift every being irrespective of their current circumstances. How could Buddha and Christ be so compassionate and loving to everyone including their enemies? **What did they love in the people who hated them?**

Inspired beings draw tremendous strength by aligning themselves to the force of truth. Their love isn't subject to change based on the behavior and thinking patterns of an individual. Buddha and Christ loved their enemies because they found them worthy of love. They discovered that their foes were human beings first and enemies later. The spirit of Buddha and Christ was wide and deep enough to recognize the greatest secret: **That which took the form of hatred in the minds of their enemies had become the cause for abundant love in their own being.**

Buddha and Christ had the spirit to recognize the intelligence of this force, while their enemies could not.

Why do we hate someone? Because our love is subject to change. Our power of reasoning stops us from loving someone as they are. Our consciousness isn't broad enough to look beyond the circumstances and the actions of an individual. The majority of human beings don't love. They only attempt to love. It's only inspired beings who can love because their love isn't subject to change. Their love is driven by a force far superior than the power of instincts and reasoning.

### The Great Discovery (The Veil of Truth)

■■■■■■■■■■■■■■■■■■■■■■■■■■■■■■■■■■■■■■■■■■

*The great men think, and you and I also think. But there is a difference. We think and our bodies do not follow. Our actions do not harmonise with our thoughts. Whatever they think must be accomplished. If they say "I do this", the body does it. Perfect obedience. You can think yourself God in one minute but you cannot be God. That is the difficulty. They become what they think. We will become only by degrees.*

Swami Vivekananda

■■■■■■■■■■■■■■■■■■■■■■■■■■■■■■■■■■■■■■■■■■

Krishna, Buddha and Christ meditated on the force of truth. They were aware of the limitations of the power of reasoning and they knew that the external world is only a dull reflection of our inner state of mind. So they chose to direct all their energies inwards and thus discovered some amazing secrets of the workings of the human mind - **that the greatest difficulty of becoming or staying inspired is our inability to stay alert.**

## The Power of Staying Alert

Alertness is the highest conscious state a human being can ever attain. In this supreme state of realization the mind cuts through the barrier of reasoning and endless thought activity and for the first time it's able to discriminate between a thought, the feelings associated with the thought, and the present moment. The mind becomes the observer and the world of thoughts becomes the observed.

Alertness shouldn't be confused with focus, which is a mind activity that lets you place your mind exclusively on the object of your desire. Focus is all about concentration. Alertness is more powerful and superior than focus. When you're alert you can watch and observe where you focus your mind. **Alertness gives you the combined power of concentration and keen observation.**

Alertness isn't a mind activity. When you're alert thoughts no longer occupy your mind. Your mind is free, having released itself from the continuous stream of thoughts. The free mind is agile, powerful, full of strength and vigor. It no longer considers it necessary to discriminate between virtue and vice, between past and future, and between cause and effect. Rather it desires only one thing - the ability to discriminate between the real and unreal, between the preferable and the pleasurable.

The ability to stay alert is the greatest secret weapon of achieving serenity and wisdom.

## The Secret To Staying Alert: Discovering The Delimitations of the Consciousness

How did this wide, expansive, limitless and ever free consciousness become narrow, restricted, limited and bound? How did the spirit of Krishna, Christ, Buddha and other wise beings become latent in other beings? What made truth invisible and caused mankind to struggle in its pursuit?

500 years before Christ was born Buddha was born. 2000 years before Buddha was born Krishna was born and 2000 years before Krishna was born some of the most purest and noble beings on earth wrote the Vedas and the Upanishads The *Vedas* and the *Upanishads,* written by ancient Hindu sages, are ancient and sacred texts which contain the secrets to staying alert. They  provide answers to some of the

most mystical questions concerning human consciousness.

Hinduism has certain strange and distinct characteristics which only a handful of people in the world are aware of. Even the majority of Hindus are ignorant of the source of their wisdom. Note that every religion seems to be inspired by a great personality. Christianity by Christ, Islam by Mohammed, and Buddhism by Buddha. But Hinduism doesn't depend on a single personality for its truth. Just as science isn't dependent on a single scientist but stands for continuous study and discovery, Hinduism doesn't rest on the shoulders of a single character or personality. It stands for the sum total of all revelations by a succession of inspired minds. In many ways Hinduism isn't a religion but an instrument for exploring God's greatest gift to humanity.

Truth comes first and religion follows later.

The Hindu sages had only one objective- to discover the truths of the universe. Like every other discovery their search began in a very primitive form but developed an institution of love, power and peace.

**The Road From Ignorance To Bliss: How The Hindu Sages Stumbled Upon A Secret Which Led To The Most Amazing Discovery Of Human Consciousness**

The ancient scriptures of the Vedas cite that a super power called God created the universe. Many hymns and prayers were written by the Hindu sages to please this supernal power. It's important to note that the Hindu seers weren't superstitious or one sided in their search for truth. In their way they were very scientific and ready to dismiss false or misleading concepts of God and truth. With the passage of time this concept of a God or supreme entity creating this universe out of nothing seemed very fragile, and it couldn't gain acceptance by many agile Hindu minds. But as the seers' search for truth deepened they realized that this universe couldn't have been created out of nothing.

**Creation is a projection of something which already exists.**

It's matter and force that pervades this universe and this matter and force existed earlier in a fine form. The sages named matter as *Akasha* and force as *Prana*. As time passed by they discovered something even more powerful - the secrets of the universe can't be found just by understanding the process of creation. It's all about manifestation. **The beginning and the end is the same. There was nothing in the end which wasn't there in the beginning**. The effect is nothing but cause in another form. The seed can't grow into a tree unless the whole intelligence of the tree is present in the tiny seed. The cause has to contain the intelligence to produce the effect. Everything that exists in this universe has manifested out of matter (akasha) and everything that acts on matter has manifested out of force (prana).

All these discoveries, brilliant as they were, still couldn't satisfy every Hindu mind. The question arose: "Why do human beings suffer? Why is one child born healthy and to a rich family while another is born blind to a poor family? If God is all merciful and forgiving why should even one child suffer? Why is death inevitable and what happens after death? What is the ultimate goal of human life?

These questions were much pondered. Concept after concept was raised and dismissed until finally the sages made a breakthrough. They discovered the greatest flaw in their approach for a higher truth.

### The Architect's Secret

Consider an example. An architect builds a wonderful mansion. Could this mansion be considered to be the greatest and the absolute best architectural expression of the builder? Would it help us to know everything about the builder?

The builder and the mansion are two different things. The mansion is only a fair representation of the architectural skills of the builder. It's by no means the absolute best because every representation is limited by the very resources or the means through which it's developed or through which it finds expression. The resources which go into the making of the mansion- marbles, tiles, cement, and manpower act as a delimiting factor in representing the architectural brains of the builder. The mansion can reveal many qualities about the builder but it can't reveal everything because the mansion by its very nature is delimited by its very own resources.

In a similar way the secrets of the universe can't be found by observing and analyzing the various creations in this world. All observations and conclusions about this universe, grand as they might be, can't be considered to be an absolute authority about the architect of the universe. It could only be considered as a fair representation of truth. The universe and the architect of the universe are two different things. Matter and force through which the universe came into existence act as delimiting factors in representing the core essence of the architect of the universe; it can't be a means to know the ultimate truth.

**The ancient seers had established this fact long before even the word science came into existence.**

If the universe can't reveal everything about the architect of the universe then what can? If matter and force, because of their delimiting nature, can't lead us to truth, then what can?

**The Birth of Purusha (Soul)**

After decades of endless research and having exhausted all their energies in trying to seek truth in the external world the ancient Hindu sages went back to their roots. They turned their gaze inwards. They closely observed the workings of every part of the body and found out that the intelligence of the body is borrowed from the mind. They then directed all their energies into understanding the mechanism of the mind. How does the mind generate thoughts? Why is the mind powerful at one time and weak at another? Why does the mind naturally gravitate outwards instead of inwards? Is the mind the source of its own intelligence? Does the mind die when the body dies?

It should be noted that these sages were ready to dismiss their own concepts which they had worked on for many long years. They had only one objective to discover "that one thing" through which the whole universe came into existence. And they were ready to sacrifice their entire life in this pursuit.

As time passed by more seers undertook this gigantic mission of discovering the truth. They found out that the mind can't be the source of its own intelligence because it's vigorous at one time and weak at another. Anything which is subject to change can't be the source of its own intelligence. Its intelligence has got to be borrowed from something else.

In pursuit of this truth these sages sacrificed all their personal desires; they fasted and lived in caves. They breathed and lived with this idea of truth until finally one day a sage discovered the grandest secret "That which became matter and force, which then became the sun and the moon, the stars and the planets, the trees and the animals, the air and water, earth and fire, mind and body, 'that one thing' is the source of all intelligence. That one thing which fire cannot burn, the wind cannot dry, water cannot wet has its seat in every thing which pervades the universe. 'That one thing' cannot be acted upon by anything. It is the source of all intelligence. He shines everything else shines"

This "one thing" can't be touched, seen, or heard. It can only be acknowledged in the highest state of alertness and realization. The Hindu sages had discovered the ultimate unity --- "that one thing" from which everything else manifests. They named it the *Purusha* (soul).

■■■■■■■■■■■■■■■■■■■■■■■■■■■■■■■■■■■■■■■■■

*Science is nothing but finding the unity. As soon as science would reach perfect unity, it would stop from further progress, because it would reach the goal. Thus chemistry could not progress farther when it would discover one element out of which all others could be made. Physics would stop when it would be able to fulfill its services in discovering one energy of which all the others are but manifestations, and the science of religion becomes perfect when it would discover Him who is the one life in a universe of death, Him who is the constant basis of an ever-changing world, One who is the only*

*Soul of which all souls are but delusive manifestations. Thus is it, through multiplicity and duality that the ultimate unity is reached. The Hindu sages had discovered the grand truth- the ultimate unity – the Purusha (soul) and could go no further. They had reached their goal.*

Swami Vivekananda

■■■■■■■■■■■■■■■■■■■■■■■■■■■■■■■■■■■■■■■■ı

As more true seekers discovered this elemental truth the question was put forth: How do ordinary beings living in the midst of worldly things perceive and live up to this transcending truth?

## The *Illusionary Power Of Maya*

The Hindu sages had discovered that a crowded mind acts as a delimiting factor in discovering the liberating truth. The power of this massive consciousness was always there within every being. It only appeared to be hidden. Note as well that these Hindu sages were studying every aspect of human behavior centuries before the birth of Christ and Buddha.

■■■■■■■■■■■■■■■■■■■■■■■■■■■■■■■■■■■■■■■■ı

*Consider this example: The farmer is irrigating his field. Through a little corner of his field he brings water from a reservoir. He has got a little lock that prevents the water from rushing into his field. When he wants water he has to simply open the lock, and in rushes the water of its own power. The power has not to be added. It is already in the reservoir. So everyone one of us, every being has as his own background such a reservoir of strength, infinite strength, infinite purity, infinite bliss and existence—only these locks in the form of bodies and minds are hindering us from expressing what we really are to the fullest.*

**Swami Vivekananda**

■■■■■■■■■■■■■■■■■■■■■■■■■■■■■■■■■■■■■■

The mind is the center of all activity, and the mind is powerful at one time and weak at another. **Notice that when you sign a cheque for a big amount you're extremely alert,** but this level of alertness may not be maintained when having dinner with your family. When men and women talk with people they're attracted to the level of alertness can be very low. When couples love each other their alertness level goes rock bottom. These ancient Hindu sages studied every aspect of human behavior and found out that many daily activities hindered one's capacity to stay alert. They termed these activities as "Maya" – that which blocked one's vision of truth. Maya stands for all those pleasurable things which become the very cause for our inability to explore our own consciousness.

Based on this truth, the seers advised people "**to give up the pleasurable and hold on to the**

**preferable."** You'll find the same truth echoing in every major religion even thousands of years later.

*Blessed are they who are pure in heart for they shall see God,* said Jesus Christ

*Beware O Arjuna lust and anger are great enemies. They cover the knowledge of even the wise*, said Krishna to Arjun in the Bhagavad Gita.

Buddha said: *When I left the palace, my father (the king) was told that I was doing a great wrong in renouncing the family. My parents, kinsmen and others tried to put pressure on me to return to the ties of family life. These wrong efforts on their side made me more determined to pursue the spiritual path. In the quest for spiritual peace several ordeals have to be overcome. Today I have found the Truth about life. What is it? The sanctification of the five senses is the way to Truth. If the senses are polluted, of what avail are spiritual exercises? When the water in a tank is polluted, all taps will only give polluted water. Your heart is the tank. When it is filled with good thoughts and feelings, all that comes out of the senses - your speech, your vision, your actions - will be pure.*

**Purity isn't about refraining from doing certain things; rather it's about living that life which helps you to stay alert and discover the liberating secrets of the universe.**

The Hindu sages were never for any prohibition. They only placed certain realities before the world after they had observed and tested it thoroughly. Their message was: Choose and indulge in activities that increase your level of alertness. When given a choice between the pleasurable and the preferable, choose the latter.

What began as a search for truth in the form of an external God sitting in heaven ended with the profound discovery of Purusha (soul) seated in every being in the universe. "He conquers all who conquers the Self. Know this and never yield" was the great message of the ancient seers. Long before any religion was born this truth was established in the Vedas and the Upanishads. Subsequently, this sublime truth set the stage for Krishna, Buddha, Christ, Mohammed, Ahura Mazda, Jehovah, Guru Nanak, and many others. Each of these imposing figures possessed all the qualities and characteristics of "that one thing." That soul which the Vedas and Upanishads claimed to be the seat of all truth was found shining in its true form in all these great characters. All the great religious figures were the highest manifestations of that grand truth which was boldly proclaimed in the Vedas and Upanishads.

The Bible, The New Testament, The Old Testament, The Quran, The Dhammapada, and every other great scripture doesn't contradict the Upanishads and Vedas; rather they fulfill it. **Each of these great scriptures might not talk about the Purusha (soul) but each and every scripture talked about the characteristics of this soul through their religious figure.**

It's knowledge that leads us to inspiration and it's character that embellishes our desire in search for this truth. Meditation leads to realization of your own purusha or soul, the key to inspiration and an inspired

consciousness. Let us all meditate on that divine truth… that ultimate unity..

■■■■■■■■■■■■■■■■■■■■■■■■■■■■■■■■■■■■■■■

*The greatest thing is meditation. It is the nearest approach to spiritual life- the mind meditating. It is the only moment in our daily life that we are not at all material – the Soul thinking of Itself, free from all matter- this marvelous touch of the Soul ! May He who is the Purusha of the Hindus, the Ahura Mazda of the Zoroastrians, the Buddha of the Buddhists, the Jehovah of the Jews, Mohammed of the Muslims and the Father in Heaven of the Christians, give strength to you to carry out your noble idea!.*

Swami Vivekananda

■■■■■■■■■■■■■■■■■■■■■■■■■■■■■■■■■■■■■■

**God's Divine Plan For Human Beings**

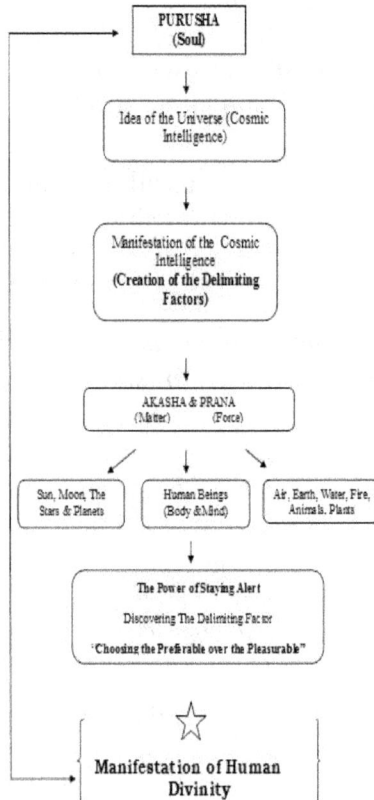

```
                    ┌──────────────────┐
           ┌────────│   PURUSHA        │
           │        │   (Soul)         │
           │        └──────────────────┘
           │                 │
           │        ┌──────────────────┐
           │        │ Idea of the Universe (Cosmic
           │        │      Intelligence)        │
           │        └──────────────────┘
           │                 │
           │        ┌──────────────────┐
           │        │ Manifestation of the Cosmic
           │        │      Intelligence
           │        │ (Creation of the Delimiting
           │        │       Factors)           │
           │        └──────────────────┘
           │                 │
           │        ┌──────────────────┐
           │        │ AKASHA & PRANA    │
           │        │ (Matter)  (Force) │
           │        └──────────────────┘
           │           ↙     ↓     ↘
```

| Sun, Moon, The Stars & Planets | Human Beings (Body & Mind) | Air, Earth, Water, Fire, Animals, Plants |

The Power of Staying Alert

Discovering The Delimiting Factor

"Choosing the Preferable over the Pleasurable"

☆

**Manifestation of Human Divinity**

## Exercise No 1

## How To Visualise Like A Zen Monk

Go to bed early and wake up early next morning. Thank the universe for a good night's sleep. Feel happy that something magical is going to happen today. Feel excited that you have got another opportunity in the form of a brand new day to express your individual clarity of mind and purpose. Feel powerful by remembering that the past really doesn't matter when it comes to changing your life. What matters is knowledge, attitude and the ability to manifest your inner strength. Close your eyes and reflect upon the sublime truths presented by seers and religious leaders. Feel inspired being in their mental presence. Be in this nostalgic moment for a while.

Then walk around your home. Enjoy silence. Take pleasure in the calmness accompanying your breath. After a while sit down in your favorite place. Sit erect and enjoy the rhythmic balance of your posture. Slowly breathe in and slowly breathe out. **As you breathe in imagine that all the qualities of those figures you worship and respect are gradually entering your being.** Feel your own power rising. Experience the love blossoming. As you breathe out imagine ignorance, in all its forms, disappearing from your self. It's all about cleansing your mind. Continue breathing in and breathing out for a short while.

Then take a notepad, open a new page and divide this page into two. Write "My Morning Experience" on the left hand side of the page and "Notes about my morning experiences" on the right hand side of the page".

| My Morning Experience | Notes about my morning experience |
|---|---|
| | 1) |
| | 2) |
| | 3) |

How was the whole morning experience? What did you enjoy the most? What did silence whisper into your ears? What secret message did you take in as you breathed in? What did you manage to throw out as you exhaled? How was your connection with your inner self? Write down all these experiences on the right hand side of the page under the heading "Notes about my morning experience". Put your entire mind into this activity. You can write, draw, or do anything that you wish on that blank notepad. It's your canvas for exploring the highest truth. Write your heart out. Don't be afraid of what you write or draw. It isn't what you write that's important but who is writing that's critical. Let your heart write and you'll win.

After writing, close your eyes and remain silent for a few minutes. Now look at your notepad again. Notice that the right hand side of the page is filled with either words or pictures which expressed or represented your morning experience. The left hand side is blank.

| My Morning Experience | Notes about my morning experience |
|---|---|
| | 1) |
| | 2) |
| | 3) |

Now carefully observe your notepad and ask yourself this question.

1) What is the difference between "Notes about my morning experience" and "My morning experience?" Are they both the same?

Look at the left hand side of the page. It's blank and yet complete in itself. Your morning experience was comprehensive. It didn't require any expression or representation to justify itself. It stands independent of any depiction.

Now look at the right hand side of the page. The moment you expressed your experience in words or pictures the experience got diluted. The absolute became the relative. The whole became the part. Your notes about your morning experience can't be considered to be an absolute replica of the real experience you went through. Your notes could only be considered to be a fair representation of your experience.

Ponder over this great reality. What made the absolute relative? What caused your experience to get diluted? Close your eyes. Breathe slowly. Think sharply. **Your own words turned your absolute experience into a relative one.** Your own expression turned the whole into part.

Look at the left hand side. It's blank. That's the truth you have to meditate on. Words and expressions act as a delimiting factor and dilute the truth. Close your eyes and contemplate on "that one thing" in you from which the whole universe manifests. Concentrate on the marvel of your deepest consciousness.

■■■■■■■■■■■■■■■■■■■■■■■■■■■■■■■■■■■■■■■■■■■■■■

*That which is nearest is least observed. The Soul is the nearest of the near, therefore the careless and unsteady mind of man gets no clue of it. But the man who is alert, calm, self-restrained, and discriminating, ignores the external world and diving more and more into the inner world, realizes the glory of the Soul and becomes great.*

Swami Vivekananda

## Exercise No 2

## How To Solve The Most Pressing Problem In Your Life?

Imagine the following scene:

A little fish wants to flee from its enemies in the water. How does it do so? Imagine that this tiny fish is going to die the next moment as a big fish is about to eat it. What could be the last thought of the little fish? Think about some possible solutions.

. . . . . . . . . . . . . .

. . . . . . . . . . . . . .

**THE FISH THOUGHT:**

**"If I had known how to evolve wings and become a bird I could have flown from the enemies in the water"**

**Notice carefully what the little fish thought. It said "If I could evolve wings and become a bird I could fly ". It didn't say that it wanted to get rid of all the big fishes surrounding it or change the immediate environment in the water. It was interested in its own evolution.**

**Moral: The fish didn't change the water or the air; the change was in itself. Change is always subjective.**

There are two aspects to every problem:

a) The subject which is "You".

b) The object - the environments and the circumstances limiting or confusing your options.

**You can't conquer all the objective environments.** You can't get rid of every person, problem and every uncomfortable event that you encounter in your life. So what do you do?

Like the little fish you evolve wings and become a bird.

### You "Take Mental Flight!"

Now take a brand new notepad and write down your most pressing problem in life. Think about all the possible solutions which will help you overcome this problem and jot them down as honestly as you can. When you write be as wicked as you can. Be as loving as you can. Write with anger. Write with wisdom. Write with love. Feel for the problem. Cry when you write. Pray when you write. Put your entire mind, body and soul into this activity. List down all the possible solutions neatly in the notepad. Then gently close your eyes, take a deep breath, hold it for a few seconds, and let it go. …How does it feel?

Now pick up your notepad and tear off all the pages which you just finished writing. Hold the ball of paper in your hand for a minute, crush it, and throw it in the dustbin.

Now sit in an erect posture with both your legs folded. Relax and breathe normally. Gently close your eyes and bring both your palms together like offering a prayer. Place a kiss on both your palms. Breathe slowly. Enjoy your breathing. Focus on the gentle rhythm of your breathing. Watch as a strange wave of calmness emerges from deep within as your breathing gets softer and softer, milder and milder. Take pleasure in this moment. Now roll back into time and imagine the happiest moment in your life. How pleased you were? How calm you were? How much fun you had? No worries, no anxiety, all enjoyment. Who made you happy? Who put a smile on your face? Dive deep into your being and bring back all those memories to the surface. Enjoy the moment.

Now open your eyes and relax. Breathe normally. Enjoy the serenity and calmness of the moment. Take pleasure in the peace permeating your being. Be in that space for a while. **Then write only one specific action step relating to your most pressing problem which you will put into practice immediately.** This specific action step could be either a physical activity in terms of getting something done or a mental attitude which you will assume towards a person or event. Be bold enough to practice what you write. Don't worry if you face problems along the way. You'll always get an opportunity to refine your action step as you progress.

Allocate some time each day to sit quietly and imagine how the little fish could have evolved into a bird. How you could take mental flight no matter how serious your problem is. Write your feelings and or solutions about the problem. Every time that you write put your heart and soul into the activity, and then in the end tear off that page and crush it.

**You should have the strength to observe your best ideas being crushed with your own hands**.

When you do this something magical will happen. If there is real power in your ideas, they will emerge in a much better, more refined, and more simplistic manner. The thought itself will have sufficient momentum to manifest the desired results with very little human effort.

**Changes will happen very quickly when you're able to facilitate even a slight shift in your consciousness**.

When your spirit soars the confusion and mental restlessness about the uncertainty of an event gradually gives way to something far superior. A power of peace and calmness gradually emerges from deep within and becomes your primary source of contact for all matters concerning your well being.

The fastest and quickest way to change is to take mental flight. Raise your spirit. Soar high. The fish in you should become the
bird. That's the only way. Always remember that the universe is waiting with all its might and strength to lend you a helping hand. Embrace it wholeheartedly and watch as power, peace and prosperity bless your life.

## Exercise No 3

## How To Express Your Love Without Being Attached.

Wake up a couple of hours before sunrise. Exactly ninety minutes before sunrise sit erect in a quiet place facing the east. The next forty eight minutes is going to be your best opportunity to manifest the divinity within you. This forty eight minutes (assuming the sun rises at 6.30 a.m. where you live the time from 5.00 am to 5.48 a.m.) is considered the most auspicious time in the whole day. Many great men and women have called this forty eight minute period "The Time of God." Those who meditate at this time achieve their latent soul power.

Now close your eyes and meditate on the word "Love." What are the pictures that flash before your eyes? What thoughts occupy your mind? Go deeper. What does love really mean to you? Does it signify someone caring for you, someone being kind to you, someone whom you could share your dreams, your grief, your likes and dislikes? Hold on to these thoughts and travel with them.

Now flash black into memory and try to recall the first time you felt the need to seek love outside of you. Did you feel powerful or pleasurable when you first went out to seek love? Be honest when you contemplate these questions. What would you have preferred amongst these two choices- a) To seek love in someone you adore; or b) to distribute your abundant love to your close ones? Which of these two options befit your real personality?

Did Christ and Buddha seek love or did they distribute their love to every single person they came across? Was their love ever limited, selfish, and centered around just a few people? **How could they love without being attached?** How could they transcend pleasure so easily and effortlessly? What did they knew about love that you are not aware of?

Meditate on the mind set of Buddha and Christ. Feel warmth and peace rising within you. Reflect on what could be the best vehicle to express your love. Is it the mind, the body, or is it something else? Is love a thought or is it an act; or is it something deeper? What happens when you express your love through the medium of body and mind? Do you limit your capacity to love every time that your love originates from the body and the mind? Do you feel the need for a superior channel to express your love without getting attached?

How did Buddha love? How did Christ love? How did Krishna love? Meditate on that pure love. Concentrating on realizing this greater love should be the direction of your meditation.

Keep your eyes closed, sit erect, and fix your mind on the lower back of your spine. Put your entire mind, body and soul on the lower back of your spine and reflect on the greatness of your being. Say to yourself:

*That power that became Buddha, That love that became Christ, That wisdom that became Krishna, I am that Power and that power exists in me. That light that shines brightly in the serene face of Buddha, Christ, Krishna and other great figures has its root on the lower back of my spine.*

Reflect on that effulgent light. Bring all the powers of your mind to rest on that light and then imagine this light shooting up from the lower back of your spine all the way to your brain center. This is the love that meditation can bring to you

## Exercise No 4

■■■■■■■■■■■■■■■■■■■■■■■■■■■■■■■■■■■■■■■

Print this poem and read it once before you start your daily meditation.

■■■■■■■■■■■■■■■■■■■■■■■■■■■■■■■■■■■■■■■

### The Force of Truth

*Who filled the space between the earth and the sky?*
*Who made sound travel through air?*
*Who gave form to fire and taste to water?*
*Who caused life on earth to be joyful and painful?*
*That force you meditate on.*

*Who caused the mind to reason and the body to be instinctive?*
*Who introduced suffering in the mind and pleasure in the body?*
*Who invented desire in my thoughts and energy in my body to fulfill the wants?*
*Who made my mind so emotional and my body so ignorant?*
*That force you meditate on.*

*Who taught me to discriminate between the good and the bad?*
*Who instructed me to choose the right over wrong?*
*Who prompted me to embrace knowledge inspite of ignorance?*
*Who inspired me to love more and hate less?*
*That force you meditate on.*

*Who made me fall for worldly attraction and rise up to Godly love?*
*Who helped me forget my intelligence and remember my divinity?*

*Who transpired to crush my purity and inspire my inner beauty?*
*Who shielded my veil of ignorance and opened up my doorway to knowledge?*
*That force you meditate on.*

*Truth is the name of that force*
*Inspiration is the fuel to that force*
*Knowledge is the guide to that force*
*Love is the strength of that force*
*That force let us all meditate on.*

## Exercise No 5

## How To Quickly Overcome Your Weakness & Improve Your Strengths

You can do this exercise anytime when calm and peaceful. Take a notepad, open a new page, and divide this page into two. Write "My strengths" on the left hand side of the page and "My weakness" on the right hand side of the page".

Write down three things you're very good at on the left hand side of the page. They could be activities or accomplishments which give you the greatest joy. It really doesn't matter if these activities aren't appreciated by your close ones, families and friends. What matters is your attitude toward these activities or accomplishments.

Now close your eyes and meditate on the satisfaction you feel when involved in these three activities. Be in this nostalgic moment for a while. Now bring both your hands together like offering a prayer and thank the universe for giving you an opportunity to express your divinity through these three activities.

Now write down three things you're horrible, or not so good at, on the right hand side of the page. These can be things you want to improve but keep failing to accomplish.

Be honest when you write. Now close your eyes, sit erect, and reflect on the first weakness. What makes you feel weak about this subject? Is it your inability to overcome the obstacle or lack of superior strength to conquer the barrier? Observe your weakness carefully. See that you feel weak because you lack superior strength. This is the truth. **It isn't the weakness which is your problem; it's the absence of acknowledging the superior force within you which is the main cause of all the difficulty.**

Open your eyes and glance at the left hand side of the page. How could those three activities make you strong, powerful and happy if strength, power and happiness never existed in you? What is the source of that joy and contentment and from where did they all manifest?

| My strengths | My weakness |
|---|---|
| 1) XXXXXXXXX | 1) XXXXXXXXX |
| 2) XXXXXXXXX | 2) XXXXXXXXX |
| 3) XXXXXXXXX | 3) XXXXXXXXX |

Close your eyes and reflect on that force which became strength on the left hand side of the page and weakness on the right hand side of the page. If strength is part of your personality then weakness can't be real. It only exists to help you find your real strength. The moment you align yourself to a superior strength, weakness disappears. Weakness has a limited existence and doesn't befit your character and persona.

**Bow down before the force which made you feel weak and pray for strength and upliftment.** Meditate on the force which made you feel strong. Keep your attention centered on "that one thing" from which the whole universe manifests. Don't despair if weakness seizes you. It will disappear just as quickly as darkness vanishes on the advent of light. You are the light of the universe. The pride of the cosmic consciousness. All strength, love and radiance reside in you.

Bring in the light. Bring in the love. Bring in the knowledge. Bring in everything that inspires and motivates you. Drive out everything that doesn't represent and befit you. Now open your eyes, and cross off everything that you wrote on the right hand side of the page.

| My strengths | | My weakness |
|---|---|---|
| 1) XXXXXXXXX | | 1) XXXXXXXXX |
| 2) XXXXXXXXX | | 2) XXXXXXXXX |
| 3) XXXXXXXXX | | 3) XXXXXXXXX |

Close your notepad and you're done.

Do this exercise as often as you can and you'll find a strange power rising with you.

After you finish this exercise print and read the below poem "Peace" by Swami Vivekananda

## "Peace" by Swami Vivekananda

*Behold, it comes in might,*
*The power that is not power,*
*The light that is in darkness,*
*The shade in dazzling light.*

*It is joy that never spoke,*
*And grief unfelt, profound,*
*Immortal life unlived,*
*Eternal death unmourned.*

*It is not joy nor sorrow,*
*But that which is between,*
*It is not night nor morrow,*
*But that which joins them in.*

*It is sweet rest in music;*
*And pause in sacred art;*
*The silence between speaking;*
*Between two fits of passion --*
*It is the calm of heart.*

*It is beauty never seen,*
*And love that stands alone,*
*It is song that lives un-sung,*
*And knowledge never known.*

*It is death between two lives,*
*And lull between two storms,*
*The void whence rose creation,*
*And that where it returns.*

*To it the tear-drop goes,*
*To spread the smiling form*

*It is the Goal of Life,*
*And Peace -- its only home!*

www.ingramcontent.com/pod-product-compliance
Lightning Source LLC
Chambersburg PA
CBHW060539030426
42337CB00021B/4344